DROPOUT

Camilo Roldán

ORNITHOPTER PRESS   PRINCETON

First Edition

Published by Ornithopter Press
www.ornithopterpress.com

ISBN 978-1-942723-06-6

LCCN 2019900605

Cover images: recto and verso of *Entropía*
(13 x 17 cm mail envelope, vinyl lettering, linseed oil)
by Francisco Lozada, 2019. Courtesy of the artist.

Design and composition by Mark Harris

CONTENTS

DROPOUT

VERRAZZANO NARROWS

        having been muggy day
                        my head wet saxophone
busking on typical
                promenade a spectral

    color-bridge flush
            with surface and waves
            at me toward the vault
        reflecting the notion

                a conglomerate of lights
                arrange to delineate
    prow   tower and stern
        cargo-ship steadily

        and a slip out of night
        as it enters through penumbra
            the notion intensified
forgotten by the time

            I get home
            that as I approach
remembered when today
                the same ship left

the notion intensified with proximity
                to the pastime
        of cataloging
            AA56

            GN54
            ML83
            OB30
            ALL

but all of these are taken
    from Ian Hamilton Finlay
and I struggle to deny
    cars on the Bay Pkwy

apart from fishing line zip
whose radio plays   the notion that
       I must leave
       and keep going

AUBADE
  for K

      heroic tennis ball
mock mock
      mocking castles down to
   war upon the salable

         to have their song
(sunshine thinking of night)
            keep a space station head
   full of dolphins

   orbiting   in pursuit
      find oneself pursued
      suddenly the heart of a cult
               beloved

         for clandestine postal service
               interstellar
         mythological squirt
Apollonian   with dolphins

               dreamboat
      angel of a racket
      "angel in German"
Guten Morgen Sonnenschein!

                index finger of Manhattan
        —the you are here
                    of touching
            map to folding map

    brought
                    rain or
                the inverse
            both   causal—

            wakes   drizzly
                    then heavier
            as if upset skies
                would sleep and would

    a rule break
                    slapping just
            wet package here
            deliver not

            window
            skyed
                New York rain
        documents

            reels and reels
    scotch-taped   torn
                shelves higher
            from floor

        to escape what bulbs
                        not whom
                but stays if
                    arch whole

wanting to consult
          poems lighten
about Joe Brainard
          —good job

MEMO

from   to not be the one on drugs
to   lithium on / lithium off
          she loves me / she loves me not
            red line / red line

            draw yourself
      prized myself for you
         drawn a heart-shaped fan
to break the hot

         cereal image bowl   half-expecting
horses   like children
       think to be noble   —nope
            beer bottle (full)

         wall of hexagons
     try to say honey   bloom
overnight   a flush
        a pink paragon

      you the olive nipples
   beer bottles   (we drank it all)
       refracted
         wake us both

     childish
     sewn together
     paisley cut-ups
naked / modeling youth

           fallen agape
        up at self
     granted to fill it
        up in me

stomach
still pressing
as though
correspondent

PICARESQUE EPISODE

surfer
    in and out of
            pouring
        pint glasses'

            pouring
        (chased waves under-
    tow forward
                as forward goes

                back as a pun on
        reluctant
            qualities of a season
        in the wrong month)

                            ice cold
                beer against brow
        have get
                before it cloy

                before it cloud—
                    what heat!
                L-I-T-E
            nor all the people

        neither all the letters
                of a so-so wave
            slapstick spilled
                torso

            rather known
    as a sign that things
            have ended
            have get

O COLORITMO

    after Alejandro Otero

     up international

              highrise stairwell

coffeepot coffeepots

         as diamonded

    from the miner's hand

          it percolates

     hospitable birds

     through sunrise

    international style   a bush

        in geometry

      not uncomfortable

      a bird percolates

     up intentional

          hairpin stairwell

out of diamonded

        Orinoco

    a bird appears

       to be orthogonal

  between as in

      the courtyard wall

   disappears

      interpersonal

           hothouse

    a bird through

every gushing rapid
hears the tide complete
    the moon as moon
                of silence

    asking what I do
replaces all
                keyboard keys
        with photos

    "Oh
        you're the Nadaísta
        who smokes
        therefore he is"

quotes to me
    my dream
        and I say
                R

    moon doth wane
        in letter
wrong as face
        in book

            will appear
    when to pulverize
            voice   what is left
        is neither

    mere noise
            nor arbitrary
                    pure elements
disappears

        through
I could say   X
     (Coyolxauhqui)
I too serve a purpose

     lemon into ocean
ripples
     young Leopardi
  alone

I could say
        P
and the moon
     would appear

  M for space
   or A
       for questions
  N for Nada

C C C
  waxing C
    laughing C
  waxing O

TRANSLATIONS OF SENTIMENTAL LUNARY
from Leopoldo Lugones' "Lunario Sentimental"

moon
     sugar in a teacup
     of celestial light
whom feeds a passion

                 nothing lascivious
hypochondriac soaking biscuit
          in the bilious mundane
chimeric mistress number

zero   (in these words
                 a cheese
spread from her category
         smooth)

née foie gras
           in the shape of an
egg   hatches oviparous deity
        a plump goose among

her goslings who   likewise
are their own bread crumbs
    a-twinkle in
              perpetual peck—

     this owl with eyes of stock
     in which a legume stews
lentil of an immense
pendulum spreading over rice

     hysterically morbid asparagus
uprooted
        by the lymphatic misery
        of a cough

skewed bone
jumping rhomboid
                    lean leg of pork
            offered as   penitence

through eons of exposure
                            slides into
        chunks
                of gelatine

to the maximum
                    weight in tapioca
        that one mule can shoulder
            @ (called

arroba) meaning
            with a holographic digestif
pearly refraction
            measures out   all on the table

        (plate of yellow snapper
                        shifts to green
ladle at rest
            in a punch bowl of blue flash)

pearl earring in the lobe   of a deaf universe
        dissolves in vinegar
        diffuse in everything
and then as if put to a dare

        I caustic moon
                to prove a point
        (that I will spend this much)
                    drink my pearl

big as double
            bass with sprezzatura she
usurps the whole
        canvas   we kneel

"poetess in French"
        not Miró's judgment
—Spanish I   long E—
            merely declension

            dolloping / her a scoop
    a dollop is
                vain ingots
                        per ignotius

each glimmer   gunshots
        dentata   bow ties hourglass   —oh
            to've been acquainted
        to be   such quaint!

        dub me as
    I'm asterisk
                contra-fascist
            bookshelves too!

goodbye
            it's been "awkward
        in Spanish"   kiss on the cheek
                        for me red

okays no   flickering red
        ribbons unfurling
            I'm all yours
        babooshka   babooshka-ya-ya

THE BEATNIK BOMKAUF

Dear Bob
        you won the games at
  San Francisco   1950s
          and that's a thing

substituted by   jazzless yawn
       of the cratered hue
          whose crackling blue
     footprintism   did set

     who died crackling blue
   whipped up   round calves
         stolen grapes   pressed until
       no one remembers

     who died of peyotl
  overdose   juxtafloating
        abomunist derelict
         above corpse

somnifluorescent
           on me
    in dabs   in ribs
   tonight I am a tent

when your wife kicks you out
when your apartment burns down
     sleep in my
     sierra of Zs

color in a food
that cannot help
            but evoke
—plus the name

                    of said color—
better than honey or milk or
pie if I were to say dream
            don't you cry

farewell's
            laughter muddled instant
                    (*carpe diem*   *mañana*)
            bored crow's nest

    getting built highway-ropes
            through my bosses
    not me
            living regret   all squirrely

buckled and kush in my
                    me ipse exprimo
        whatever years of thong
            gives a lariat goddamn

            would rather live and let
        deliquesce—a quart—
        smeared   (glimpsed)
                        in orts

from the gin effervestibule
        a question-mark neck
        or a whale
                all blueberry

wepa!   horripilate
                        skinflint
          goosebump in your bland
          curling dark   intoxicate

          decline
(rich with paupers bluffing)
                        of the modern state
          you joust   —wepa!

     no thanks   no Hapsburg
          self-parody
codpiece nor
          saddle horn of

bronco bucks
                insistent wepaholic
     reared performance
          of the tough

          bacon windmill
          about and aboutness
     to assay
                        pancaked   (wepa!)

          on the vain iron
skillet shield
          eggs to begin
                little birds in circles

HEAD WITHOUT A TORSO
after Amílcar Osorio

always larger in thought
        than what is here
    outside the Met
            remembering while

            Bach Inventions
    for saxophone
            play our discrete anachronism
            that we

    wandered around looking for
Satyr Playing a Double Flute
        with arms   hands
        and remnants of

                instrument
yet could not find
            what in truth
        is only

        a chipped head
            puffed-out cheeks
    two equal sized lacunae
        between pursed lips

gust
newspaper
in place
against a fence

yellow
leaden
marginal bivouacs
wrinkled

tedious furrow
yonder loose
if chain-
linked

reap   —remember
there're boys there
nightly
sup and yield—

breeze resisting
practice
moves eventually
itself spherical

to shred
on barbed-wire
tattoo
(false impasse)

topple
backwards
over huge radish
up out of the ground

AUBADE
for J

       breakfast under tree
front-yard center
                      small table coffee
           fruit in yogurt

          wanton
             hunger
   sent
long walks with a big hound

        and gone
       western
            a poet in the dark becomes
            a poet among poets

frogs croaking
          sameness at dawn
   a frog
              wriggles out of palm

        fingers limp
     without a plan
                 bereft
hound seeking in the wet grass

THE PACHUCO AS DAFFODIL
after Octavio Paz

transpontine bridge
        crossed me
    wrung my waist
      a breeze over image

    no star but what I caught
        reflected in water—
    a cup is
    a yellow cup

orchard
            path
    clouds
        papaya flesh

            burst
    of glass
            in the desert
    as firing range

        freak snowstorm
hispid plants   white
        memory
                    cellophane

VERRAZZANO NARROWS

something a pylon is
            about a span
                    sometimes
        in the cables

as a person jogging to the stern
                of a tanker
        suspends
            if one be stationary

    as it passes
    when looking through it
        a curving fence
        becomes two fences

                before a tulip
        stem in May
                go unnoticed
        by picnickers who

    slack or taut
            swell
                    in motion
        again

    up from anchor
through surface
            into ship's bow   (shine)
                to link   (to clack)

        flattering to sum of speech
    (kite syntax   flutters)
                to seem to speak
        when looked at

sustaining
      bowl of grapes
      blue
pendant

      bow
         string perpendicular
crossing itself   again
         A sharp

      pylon bloodied
a tulip
         steps on the crescent
      of its former self

LA TORRE

This card the mouth
calligraphic

has from between
star and devil

fallen agape
up at self who

says it better
to say no thing

not only flow-
ers but stones if

you must then feel
the lead measure

contuse a form
minor but bald

as on tires we
rode from one place

careful not to
to the next when

also plucked at
color lifts and

falls into an-
other as brush

mixes or knife
applied would say

the only bricks
we have are friends

here presents a
wall and such and

such a wall as
I would have you

and have you think
a crannied hole

is a lost friend
that had from it

lifted out of
road and set so

there can be a
brick in a brick

wall the eye picks
whereafter he

sat wailing on
sidewalk for all

the world we've seen
we made and broke

upon our selves
cardboard plastic

gum chewed and spat
pavement laid or

motionless wings
that are the not-

music the dead
things at the plinth

where in peals we
heard this lament

we fucked up we
fucked up and I

want to go home
I want to go

home but you know
et cetera

all a hot wind
et cetera

strangers shaking
hands in words home

hands shaking deaf
with tears mucus

run down it all
there found I held

brushes mixing
an orange with white

visage my friend
half obscured by

himself center
turning pink streaks

or vermillion
understood as

a fist of worms
in the brain a

worm in the brain
inverse image

of green drop it
the human hood

spread orange in time
teeth dead in soil

unwound to re-
corded bird song

to recorded
flute concerto

I listening
twenty years late

heard a baroque
Saraband whose

controversial
dance gave up its

feet five-hundred
years ago takes

me twenty more
years to learn right

ways of speaking
on the dancers'

mannered
swooping horns that

flash their two sides
and the dancer

who scrapes wooden
slats of his crown

in the earth like
antelope do

in a dream I
still see them when

playing wooden
nose flute a man

on the subway
car walks down and

comes back playing
harmonica

we can recog-
nate ourselves and

this family
plot that is now

cement where sits
a vibrant pain

tearful tonight
wails we fucked up

below the vine
electric voice

the morning song
we heard at night

whose cheap said cheep
and change order

from five-hundred-
seventy-six

red bricks to one
creamy F sound

a wall that falls
to extend so

I am the stone
that kills me it

drops completely
down a plumb line

tumbles through thread
recoiling at

the tip of our
furthest spiral.

These ones are trains
then crossed as twos

become oblique
heads formed ear-first

to imply a
tunnel outside

that funneling
movement walk made

certain sweeps of
people seated

would do to cut
lush a vine up

tree hits and runs
along branches

the eye follows
trained on bright cloud

blue graffiti
for an exit.

This not working
outboard motor

sits and won't rip
any pull cord

but raises it-
self trailing tail

whose definite
article the

in answer to
gentle curve banks

echo with black
sentences croaked

along river
when distracted

by fireworks re-
flection one for-

gets to j-stroke
and the canoe.

Cotton kerchief
knots recollect

a screen-printed
pattern onto

what's contently
tied out of sight

as nostalgia
for wet gray time

pulled away once
the squeegee passed

pressing lightly
and who decide

a glib morning
if it persists

all day never
fills a cup are

foxes comma
below the vine.

Kinfolk clambake
shouting watch this

with the intent
to swiftly zip

out from under
knife spoon and fork

prepositions
a checkered sheet

one rips and rips
hard at ety-

mological
edge of pattern

read family
to be the first

patron of thus
fails and launches

full silverware
set into space.

Illusion of
through arches each

He'll come along
painted to look

a space larger
while they recede

Won't say a word
like landscape dis-

towards the backdrop
than what this is

Maybe Monday maybe
proportionate

moving downstage
to a figure

The man I love
will appear as

if pasted on
To make him stay.

Squat flat slept as
matchbook stepped on

holding the wind
breaker so high

you can't grasp which
sleeve is full of

elbows the air
for the baggie

your pal's hand pats
down and swear it's

here how could I
lose my arm through

the hood facedown
grinding fabric

no pocketed
fist my heart won't

when paranoid
about the cops.

Pulp your death mask
comma no mask

if split before
yourself and gone

would suffice if
instead of a

headless paper
maché figure

a new mask built
around nothing

delimits the
wearing wet strips

hung side by side
that is parade

so startled they
quiver prepared

to cover and
show you what is

not apparent
in thinking of

a space between
pressures comma

light's narrow lines
his thousand flutes

fill a valley
with seem to be

his eye made pulp
and the gaping

visible by
his brutal head

made of wire frame
whose plucked warbling

notes are fingers
that nervously

spread open your
venetian blinds.

The time it takes
for this event

to find me is
detrimental

to itself and
is failing me.

Or the event
has been and like

post-orgasm splits
into discrete

information
sex person love

what being is is
left incomplete

y mi mal es
tan entero

I die without
and without death.

The time it takes
se me dobla

and is doubled
in duration

del evento
compartido

and because I'm
living is this

what will happen
when I so hope

you die of not
dying caught up

por enreda-
dera y la

subida que
diste para

encontrarnos
is failing me.

The time it takes
is failing me

cual vivo sin
vivir en mí

met with response
more than silence

en un gesto
repetido

shattering and
has collected

a la vez y
finalmente

erased I feel
I don't when pulled

mis romances
invisibles

in a gesture
repeated and

destrozado
recogido

all things in thirds
I found the cross

absurdo en
mi pecho tal

invisible
ballads folded

se me dobla
mi dolor y

all at once and
finally said

en respuesta
sin quietismo

do not translate
what is private

el tiempo que
dura no dá.

The time it takes
El tiempo que

is failing me.
dura no dá

something lasting.
Duraciones

sin fruto que
así dudo

what is a fruit
if not ripened.

Se me dobla
Softer softer

Dura duro
I am doubled

Muero muero
I live I live

Vivo vivo
I die I'm dead.

Bajo la vid
y la vida

Below the vine
and the life I

lower the vine
unto my life.

I said it was
a quickness hard

que cae de
la Torre y

conocemos
en ladrillos.

They were my friends
all in falling

and when we thought
we would as grapes

on the pavement
land wet instead

we land in sets
to build again.

All of this a
deck of cards launched

upwards like a
carpetbeater

thrashes a rug
gentle dust motes

are drifting cards
in play and flight.

The one one thought
to have in love

el espejo
de mí en mí

con esperan-
za de verte

ever spirals
away withal.

But it is a
structure building

the time it takes
to rise its own

collapse and one
remembers there

order always
is to the deck.

I would lament
my life if you

were to remain
here dejected

aun después que
la plomada

llegue al fin
de su cuerda

no redoblas
and you fail me.

I.

This is a poem about Lee Lozano
(1930-1999),
　　her art-
life life art, at once swan song and
owl's perspicacious eye, ruler
　　wisely cold
concerning you (false troubadour),
raucous yet discrete in turn, who
　　without prose

nor rhyme sound, was foundational,
how nothing else can now be done.
　　Despotically read,
the mystery of what Lozano might
have declared her self, her art, towards
　　her death,
speaking under shade　　of a lime tree
somewhere in Dallas, Texas, to a
　　close friend,

will never be known. Just like her
hours of conversation, what she called
　　Dialogue Piece
(1969), when artists came to her SoHo loft,
all things available, instantaneous, yet
　　of talk
no record can be found beyond someone
else's art action, someone's memory
　　of her,

or like a medieval panegyric
on the Spanish queen's favorite bookkeeper
   (the numbers
—account of acres, gold, slippers and sovereign,
     with the poet, are all today
   one piece—
gone to most   (elegant superlative
painted bodies purchased for what had been
   wisdom, future

lessons that should have been remembered,
     lip glossing over details that once
   enriched poetry
while they ravaged ramparts and cities ...),
whereas in this instance the numbers leap,
   dance, thrash,
grand jeté—clinamen of cause / effect—
brush back and forth and wander a
   New York

no longer imagined merely as decline),
this too concurrent with a definition
   of tragedy,
what philosophers tell in stories about their friends:
     perfunctory, equivocal praise,
   conditional, hidden
    by the demands of a
brutal era more the subject than any
   one person.

That is, as Lozano would have her milkshake
dissipate in flavor of the way presence
   expressed blenders,
her presence on the scene   so integral to
her absence from   official twisty-straws

of dissemination,
ostensibly writing about one subject
while keeping tabs (whole windows open)
    on another

the way someone once taught you
to savor a near distance when
    walking through
Manhattan, never making eye contact
with strangers (one questions whether this is
    really necessary,
        or if it wasn't brought
from another metropolis),
    so too

it might have been better not to speak
        sincerely of passion
    when leaving
Neukölln, queasy with a terminal kiss,
queasy on the train to the airport,
    queasy with
your first and only Europe, all your savings
sucked up in a poorly programmed trip,
    average milkshake.

Sure, it was magical, though inevitably
you rule yourself out, believe the
    Best Western
so wholeheartedly   there's no room left;
heartbroken cities medieval take a nap,
    sleepwalk through
mocking castles down to war upon the
salable fantasy, sleep cessation concrete map,
    cultish Bermuda

shorts dreamboating in shoes matched
to this tourism racket, old world singers with
　　new media
performing culture for a bot on three weeks vacation,
　　　　shibboleth spills wine on itself
　　as ignorance
　　　　of what is understood to be culture
frustratedly puked into anxious wake of
　　two years

gone by, always larger in thought　　than what was there;
thus it would have been　　you could free yourself　　had you
　　seen yourself
　　　　reunited with a ghost,
remembered laughing, had known Lozano's
　　"MAGIC WORD
TO CANCEL SPELLS […] OR, TO COUNTERACT A
WITCH'S POWER;　　YELL: ORTHOGRAPHY!"
　　Two people

are just a couple red lights　　atop each tower
in polyrhythm　　who agree to alert
　　planes flying
low, a favorite bridge (Verrazzano,
Brooklyn, Manhattan, Williamsburg,
　　Queensboro, etc.)
doesn't really matter, remembering
many years ago your walk to it,
　　determined jumper

barely derailed by the detour, cold beer
　　　(if to die it might be better
　　drunk); decide
to find a Spätkauf, buy a liter of sameness,
　　　this one memory even

fuzz uncapped
  over the Spree another glass
little more than stopped here
  because freewheel

separated from the cassette on this
   borrowed bike, rubber jam
  against frame,
staring into river's lap, feeling that you
   failed to fix your heart;
  attempted repair
of one bike, then another, vacation
   occupied, tinkering, pull
  the chain

pretending it is the cord for some steam engine's
   horn to disperse cattle who wandered
 —calm, sate—
   onto the tracks, to fill an open
seemingly fertile   midwestern pasture with
  antique whistle,
   flute of cyclopean idiot
passion misplaced in cycles of work and
  temporary liberation,

   sounding less and less like
announcement, just the mere shriek that follows
  failed endeavors,
   background noise brought
   forward by turning up the
  squelch circuit,
art of sampling reduced to minimal
   beats that back
  talksong complaints

of exploited subjects: you tried to be present.
Taking pictures all day long, for the first time
    you note
suspension cables, lights evenly spaced
along mainstays   —the deck's yellow
    streetlamps plucked
as periodically obscured by cables
from this angle walking toward the
    slurred mass

they are points that define the arc—
parabola cutaway from a cone,
    the cone
emerging from the river's chop and foam
—invisible, tilted, vertex upheld in the sky, pointing
    beyond bridge
        to an unscalable focus,
inhuman aperture   traced in human feats,
    in parabolas

        across the suspension of puns
that stretch and pierce and haunt every
    form imagined
until the roving, perforated geometries
        become so unbearably diaphanous
    to possess
and dispel the line   you pinch yourself,
construct a cone of skin,   architectural feat
    centered in

Grunewald, where today the two of you walk,
        long ago the site of a battle,
    smoke weed,
stand on the cliffside   overlooking Havel,
sloops in the sunset, jibs described as vermillion

you feel
confused about   because they were previously red,
        and whenever you read it aloud
      the sound

of this word (vermillion) reminds you of *verde*,
so you think of a pine green, forest green,
      undeniably green,
          though the word means red-orange;
thus departing from a plainer sense
      (red), you're
          overcome by its opposite (green),
flash of words a hole in the fabric of their
      canvas sails

fluttering through the mind as potential
paintings never completed, as Lozano's
      Wave Paintings'
(1969) undulant lines a mimicry
of what was to come   (wave wave wave goodbye)
      —rhythmic knowing
herself, hours carefully haptic—were a straight
          shot through   vibration, stoned
      for days,

sped-up on bennies to finish in one sitting
magnified nanometers of color—one red,
      two green,
          next one gone, stoned again—
stoned every day in protest of mastery,
      abstraction rejected,
          her own work suddenly gauche,
ruled herself out, cut holes in the canvas
      lost now,

thrown on the streets of SoHo,
draped sprawl of history, like swimming
    upside down,
quicksilver surface to look through
to better understand the purpose of
    this visit,
like looking through the infinite yet
countable latticework of a medieval
    garden wall

where you can see yourself, or someone else
    who thinks he is in love,
    sees people
fuck in the shapes and shadows,
    limbs and torsos reorganize,
    hair flows,
unsure what is or where because he never
watched other people fuck in
    real life

(only on digital screens), adjusting
his position to better view them
    through this
perforated canvas; poke a finger
to clear a leaf and realize, due to your
    shifting line
of sight, that there is a second screen
beyond the first, their vectors producing
    a third

screen of shapes in magnifying proportions,
inflating volume, a million samples of
    skin, synced
moaning and movement, or then steadying
yourself   on the wall   with both hands, face

flat against
and eye to oculus, out of a single view
so many moonbeams pour into cold flesh,
    quicksilver surface

the mirror Lozano held between her legs
to observe an art without supports, what she called
    Masturbation Investigation
(1969), wherein she records "TUMESCENCE, TURGIDITY,
COLOR CHANGE FROM LIGHT RED TO BRIGHT RED,
    VIOLENT EJACULATION
OF LUBRICATION FROM DUCT NEAR CLITORIS,
& VIBRATION DURING ORGASM," becoming
    borderless person

salty origin of all things   made public,
worlding waterfall, fountain of thought that
    never ends
but is held apart   open vulva of all
material phenomena squirting forth,
    song in
        climax   a cosmos
alluded to throughout the whole tradition of
    human joy

never caught in a snapshot. Landscape rebuilt
with bricks and remnants of what stood before
    the bombing,
what is there to find here? What is it
you think is worth talking about now?
    To seek
a herculean empathy, patience and
forgiveness for all beings—can it be built,
    this world,

this infinite utopian moment, with anyone?
        Is that love? Or is it
    always impossible
        because you believe things,
do not recognize fathomless possibility
    within you,
experience personal history as   actions
you yearn to know yet cannot share,
        cannot recall,

because of those selfsame experiences—no.
To wit: you demand to be understood, and in
        that effort
to understand, admit that you do not,
do not understand, and lose her
        in laurels.
She always mixes up the Spanish word for bear,
(*oso*) with the word for eye (*ojo*). How lovely:
        the eye

as bear endeared to the thought of pulling
gestures from a stream, arc of bridge
        cast like
fishing line to pull back   from extinction
brown bears in Grunewald, evoked with a crack
        —short whip
back to the bridge   over the Spree, their absence
        the invisibility of an eye to itself,
        ocio cultural,

arbitrarily consumed, because you don't know
the difference between Austrian and German
        culture anyway,
        so it doesn't matter
where the two of you go for dinner

when Berlin
is under construction; every museum
      you want to see
   under construction.

II.

You aspired to conquer, a Cid in Valencia,
piña Tizona in hand, but found in the dry bed
    del Turia
a colossus dead, its great conquistador's helm,
El Museo de las Ciencias Príncipe Felipe
    prostrate, aimed
at the Mediterranean, in its viscera
      an aquarium where
   a Beluga

stares into the corner, facing away from the audience
      awaiting entrance to the
   big pool
      —liberation from the usual
view of walruses neurotically swimming
    in circles—,
a tour guide who says,   *Your sovereign will*
embrace you once again; from Albufera,
    freshwater eels

travel thousands of miles to the Sargasso Sea
      with a mind for only one thing:
   thus creatures
      all, you a creature as any,
wriggle away from history on

a quest.
In Albufera the two of you wander through
brush and scrub and over the dunes to an
    empty beach,

swim naked in the Mediterranean's warm
tumult, gently spinning as a pair of
    cetaceans, looking
through the variegated surface, sunlit
lack of effort, easily pleased without
    a future
        and back in your cabin fuck.
If you have not gathered, this other woman is
    not Lozano

        and he, you, a man—Adonis!
a boy as much as anyone under thirty
    (youthful, strong,
androgynous) can be—don't be astonished:
heaven is not so distant from earth, nor snow so far
    in color
from coal   when the darts of passion lance reckless
        through the German forest,
    boars' whiskers

filtered through the treetops; abandon
roles, try to move on, to make it
    —yourself—new,
        but the old role, a shadow
cast across oneself, cuts your face into pronouns
    detectives piece
        together, who you once were
        and no longer are:
    he's dead

you say, but how can he be really—a ghost
        is alive, that life drifting as if
    impelled, inertia
of love brushing past in the hall,
arm hairs bristling beneath sudden
    cold, increasing
cold as the specter moves on, departing
from you as if a fate, your fate,
    sidestepped you,

        or you it, and now
still alive but useless as a
    bent screw.
"You are here" of touching map to folding
map innuendos' mixed-up toolbox self-image,
    Lozano's early
vulgar mockery and self-sale (1962): "COCKS!CUNTS!
TITS!BALLS!"; toilet seat painted with shit eating grin (1963),
    nightmare art

        world ascent; pencil contorted tools
(clamp, hammer, wrench, screwdriver, crowbar,
    hatchet, razorblades
(1963-64)) all in self-stimulating poses,
        red (or green), shifting like a card spun
    cages bird,
two sides converge and the pun's paired meanings
meld: "ALL VERBS," the titles of her paintings,
    are innuendo,

you are verbs in someone else's sentence, the
"REAM / SPIN / VEER / SPAN / CROSS / RAM / PEEL / CHARGE / PITCH /
    VERGE / SWITCH /
SHOOT / SLIDE / CRAM / GOAD / CLASH / CLEAVE / FETCH / CLAMP /
LEAN / SWAP / BUTT / CROOK / SPLIT / JUT / HACK / BREACH /

STROKE / STOP"
(1967). You're a tool yearning to say *I too*,
     but Lozano is not
  a touchstone

for concern and empathy; you try to eavesdrop
on her conversation, but there is
    only void
left by a woman who, in her *Boycott Piece* (1971)
      stopped speaking to other women.
    Lucy Lippard
said it was an   "eccentric" decision, equal
in eccentricity to Lozano's *Grass Piece* (1969);
    Helen Molesworth

said it felt "consummately pathological"
yet is the rejection of the intertwined systems
    of patriarchy-capitalism:
it exposes the categories man / woman
      and   "the impossibility of a
    life lived
outside the societal confines and
projections   of gender," and, doing so
    as artwork,

"refused the demand of capitalism for the
constant production of private property;"
    Cheryl Donegan
      said it was typical of '70s
American feminism to place emphasis
    on choice
      as an iteration of "self-determining
individualism" that sees "control, performance
    and self-perfection"

as paramount, that Lozano forfeited real change
        in favor of policing her "social diet;"
    Lauren O'Neill-Butler
said it may have been merely concealment of work
in progress, suggests   Lozano's notebooks be kept private;
    Sarah Lehrer-Graiwer
is the source for the Lozano of this poem—
you should probably read her book. This
    other woman

        said *I do not feel heard* because
the High Rising Terminal of her assertions
    was taken
as doubt, and you doubted her, subconsciously,
at every turn, and there's no room for that
    even if
you were to stretch time into an immense
glissando, radial, pulsating circumference
    of centerless

globular mass, electric portal through which
patience and growth strike out from earth
    emerald towers
lit by the glow of starship engines, fling
humans outward as windows open upon
    cosmic afternoons'
intergalactic aperture, pleasure cone
cruise through the rings of Saturn, beyond
    Oort Cloud

icebergs of historical subjugation, solar
        systemic violence behind you,
    aroused electrons
everywhere unobserved, no longer domestic,
photonic wellspring radical energy stream

drifting satellite,
time and time enough   to imagine and imagine
yourself elsewhere   with her   other than this
    awkward conversation,

it still wouldn't be space enough   given
your inability to listen correctly,
    handwringing over
the wrong response, what kind of silence
and how much, how best not to speak
    and respond,
who to condemn and how to laud, wondering
        how to affirmatively assert
    your silence.

Give a long pause; hope for her to speak.
        Hang it all, there can only be one
        Lee Lozano:
you are conflating them and that is unsafe,
or is it unsafe to treat a woman's experience
    as unique,
to deny the shared, or is it your desire
to ameliorate the legacy of her *Boycott Piece*
    ("pathological," "eccentric")

by setting her alongside another woman
similarly disposed, who is, though safe,
    uncomfortable (Lozano
refuses to speak). Likewise, she, feeling unheard,
has foregone speech because you are the boy
    in *Boycott.*
If all the verbs in her sentences are boys like you,
then why should she speak that grammar unto
    another woman?

Could any worthwhile gesture *not* pursue
self-perfection? Is every piece phrased in
    historical present?
        A notebook made public?
Lozano declares that women are complicit in the
    manifold fuckedness
of the fact that it becomes hard
        for her to order a cup
of coffee?

Mediterranean high-tide waves power this
        machine that records your love
    (holographic embrace),
        but another text,   not only her memory
(which includes your faults) reveals itself when
    she reads
what you can't, how this beach turned you inside out,
        why this unrequited condition befits
a cyclops.

Everything is labor except smoking, sleep and
good sex, after which she turns away from you
    because work
tomorrow intrudes, demanding rest (ok),
        but it is hard to grasp the
    emotional labor
of being held, and the blanket is too small
        and it is hers and you are cold
    and unemployed.

        Or it is then worse in dreams
when smirking she rubs herself and says,
    What's wrong,
didn't you want *to fuck me?* meant to be alluring,
but a quick willingness leaves you

ashamed, nauseated
at the grass down-pressed by your own   persistent belief
        that this should happen under
lime trees.

        Though only she can confirm it,
no rose petals could mark the spot.
        Instead, overripe
avocados tossed in a bocci ball game splattered mush
foolish words, or lack thereof, one tiny bird
        sings, *Tandaradei,*
where the tree could have been,
Tandaradei, mini-singer who tells that it was
        Brooklyn Bridge

        whose iron trellises
            crosshatched into her visage,
        smirking desirous
yet closed; satisfied by your panting idolatry,
willingness to cast yourself into the role
        she needed
and please her, yet barred from you as a person,
a galaxy in repose   to drift toward and
        leap from

as pitcher of thought pouring self into river,
        shadow-self pours into dirt:
    The Star
risen from within a skull that has become
the only stage for art, the walls of projection:
    Love Cry?
Orthography? Immortality: *"morir no puedo /
        que perdí / la vida después que /
    os vi"*

subsumed into Valencia's Francoist movies
—change the channel—TV show about animals
    who perform:
a falconer won't make it   beyond the first round;
a man with his donkey   endears the audience:
    everyone agrees
a donkey would never do those tricks,
they are obstinate, too intelligent, but people like
    you would,

        covered in olive oil from head to toe,
putting it on to dilute sunscreen, putting it on
    to treat
sunburn, putting it on for pleasure, a live
offering, sacrifice and libation for
    her fountain,
waterfall of immortality (once again to flow,
ancient river of orgasm; to leap from the crag
    and become

eagles, myth; to escape conquistadors and love)—
you grip the bridge's rail, the bike is jammed,
    memory lived
drifting out from under as what you could have said.
You watch the Spree, list the Museums under construction:
    Alte Nationalgalerie:
Bauarbeiten im Gange; Pergamonmuseum:
Bauarbeiten im Gange; Neue Nationalgalerie:
    Bauarbeiten im

Gange... ; even the path along the Spree
in Treptower Park   is under construction.
    Danke schoen!
And despite the ongoing nature of all things
(you can't leap off one night of passion twice

(*Tausend dank!*);
you cleave to the same waterfall, are cleaved),
despite supposedly reciprocal handshakes
    (*Danke auch!*)

you have demands for the world, mostly
implicit, and chief among them to
    "be loved,"
which may never be met, at least
not as one imagines it—if your friends
    are friends
they love you, but that is not
       what you wanted,
    not enough.

III.

You seem to have forgotten moments of pleasure.
Green, they were money; red, they were losing yourself.
    You seem
to have forgotten lunch on the shore of a lake.
Green, it is nature; red, it is a cherry.
    You seem
atomized, excited, radiant-energy-wave
green, a new labor, a red lunar eclipse, magic.
    You seem

lost at the bridge's rail   looking into the Spree
remembering another bridge, bigger, your self
    numerous off-ramps
a highway   silent contemplates aspirations
abandoned, hoping to find the love you sought,

unable to
concede that you found a friend   to dissuade you,
a hand on the shoulder   guiding you to the door
	through which

"DESTRUCTION OF (OR AT LEAST COMPLETE
UNDERSTANDING OF) POWERFUL EMOTIONAL HABITS.
	KEY > EMOTIONS
ARE ALSO HABITS, LIKE ANY OTHER REPETITIVE
BEHAVIOR. / I WANT TO GET OVER MY HABIT OF
	EMOTIONAL DEPENDENCE
ON LOVE." In reading the dream   you write it,
	but how should you read it?
	Not zugswang,

not chess, worn-out modernist visual metaphor?
You should find a way to write it   other than
	disaster, terminus
		for all Modern (read "Western") Art.
Do not check to see where she has gone, but trust
	she follows
through the door—but you can't help it:
queen takes bookkeeper when one defines a
	set as

"THE TOTALITY OF ALL ACTS THAT SATISFY
A GIVEN CONDITION," the condition being
	repartee consciously
thrown silk ball   until your hand stutters vagaries,
pissing yourself   because you drank too much
	Pernod, unable
to remember how you came to justify this
perpetuum mobile, counting the bounces
	without sum;

the condition being the word itself: set,
      as when you set it all aside
    for someone,
set to take a trip; set onto which walks
      a persona, typeset and ready;
    Colombian emerald,
set in a Germanic necklace; set upon which
      the game plays out, sett of a
    tartan skirt;

the condition a painting that cannot exist
      as anything other than a
    visual experience,
a lengthy peroration intended
for nothing other than the sensation
    of time;
a ubiquitous condition only
pointed to by that occasional
    shape in

the blur, return of experience had,
like a thing unsaid rose beneath
    your skin,
a tumor out of subcutaneous fat
excreted into view, nodes of
    having had
amassed, the intimate things one knows
merely that: a collection of baubles
    that plague

you; your nightmare of passion spent
      and lost recurs often:
    Berlin U-Bahnhof
where one falls slowly down, and like a turtle
flipped and spinning on its shell,

shouting *Help,*
I can't see! I'm lost! Where did you go?
when someone nearly stops to turn it
    aright, but

decides not to because—*fuck that,*
I have to get to work. On the U-bahn,
    you played
at being small, reminding her of the sorrows
tall women suffer. Now, you do not wish to say
    she's tall
because it would seem to reinforce her self-image
(do not wish she were not), but to deny her body would be
    to deny

her frustrations   with Hollywood, advertisement's targeted
        oppression. Now it is a chess board,
    a dialogue,
so you must respond (zugzwang!), yet
your complicity as the target and not
    the subject
        nullifies dismissal of the image:
you would claim to desire differently as
    a solution

but it is about her body, not about your
desires, how they guide the desperate search to
    articulate responses
that provide more than mere affirmation, support
and comfort for a person subjected daily
    to violence:
you know resistance and revolt take many forms,
but there is only one woman sitting before you.
    Trapped within

the implicit objectification of all
desire, trapped by your saccharine fantasies,
    ignorant of
her praxis, but expected to respond (zugswang!),
you have nothing worthwhile to say, and lose
    your queen.
Or maybe shutting up isn't as hard   as you wish that it were.
        Maybe listening is a thing
    that matters,

silence is a form of action, not a loss.
You pendulate between the short lyric as
    insistent compression,
long poem as extreme of   rambling insistence.
Do you tergiversate in mere aversion
    to feeling?
When Lozano cast off the art object,
she cast herself aside too, denied herself
    access, silence

deliberately increased into swell of
line-break, became a poem whose eventual
    return wrote
in 1998 her "QUESTIONAIRE, WITH JOKES, /
CONCERNING PURCHASES & PURCHASERS / OF
    MY ART."
How would you make that gesture? Who are your readers?
        How invested have they become?
    Poets, academics,

        some artists, art historians, critics
(Sarah, Laura, Cheryl, Helen or Lucy?),
    the woman
you claim to love? Lozano's ghost, mortified?
Men? An endless list of powerful men? Are they

rich? Comfortable?
Do they have real jobs? Salaries? Do they speak
        a second language? French, German
    or Spanish?

Finally put out that book, will someone teach it?
Did they read it online, or in a lit. journal
        published somewhere
            west of New York and east of LA?
Will someone review it? Will they talk about
        terrible things
you've written   over a glass or two of Pernod,
or will they talk about the terrible things
        you've done?

        Pushed to the very misanthropic,
like Tom Otterness shooting a pound dog
        "for art,"
        like Lt. Thomas Glahn, who executed
his hunting dog, Aesop, as a parting gift because
    Woman A
would not love him   and *Woman B* died
(what *was* the moral?),   does extreme
    egg extreme?

Be water, move in ever replenishing doubt.
When Lozano cast herself aside, she cast off
        the market,
gave up shows, changed her name—dropped
Lozano (née Lenore Knaster)—to become
        singular E.
E left for Dallas. E stopped making art. E
committed a form of conceptual suicide, became
        pure energy

seeping from a vent below a chasm
in her own sanctuary, inhaled deeply and spoke
    for herself,
        perhaps realized from moment
to moment   she was able to be a numinous
    "Know Thyself,"
inscribed herself (E) into the lintels above, inscribed
the stone in her life, liberated in a single notebook page:
    "<u>DROPOUT</u> <u>PIECE</u>

IS THE <u>HARDEST</u> <u>WORK</u> I HAVE EVER DONE" (1970)
and was never heard from again, or so says
    her Vida,
though she may have teetered on the outskirts
        for a lid, smoked the best of her self,
    meandered, dallied
        with the decent men she knew,
chalked up by her enemies under the coinage
    "acid casualty,"

a grid of blotter paper with UFOs or Mickey Mice
like a psychedelic chessboard that asks you to
    turn on
        the cinematic experience of perpetually
proceeding, not located in any one place,
    tune in
        to her piece, the music
of a letter E   squirting through the cosmos,
    drop out

of writing poems, reenact the nature of the original piece
        and make art your life
    on stage
with the band, even without a wifi signal,
as a letter to an old friend living in a distant land,

in transit,
two separate actions, two people are fragments
      and the only record of the gesture
    the memory.

Somewhere at the other end of all this
she sits at a desk with a headset listening
      to men
proclaim their love in the form of a customer
complaint, obligated to help them resolve
      the issue,
restart their modems, empty their browser
      caches; listens and listens to men
    recount dreams

of her, anxious to hear her proclamations,
unwilling to mute their personal problems
      long enough;
waits for the delay   caused by the satellite
connection between bumblefuck Texas
      and Germany;
listens briefly to you, and then, moving on
with her life, gently whispers her advice:
    drop out.

      As a parting gift—you
imagine all parting gifts will be held
      by recipients
forever singing your tribute, your absence—
you bought her a cactus, said to it, *thou too art,*
    oh cactus!,
      on this foreign soil,
rooted in a sandcastle, shape of a woman,
    shifting dune

punctuated by alluring grasses,
        and with that you,
    imaginary man,
sit on her alone, the monocular beast
        who blows his reeds, pining for
    an ocean
that will never congeal into the desired nymph,
        her red breasts colored by the
    setting sun

gone in a green ray. *Hacías el oso,*
        made a fool of yourself,
    circus bear
        dancing like someone shamelessly drunk,
you were drunk with wrongheaded love,
    the immense,
luminous eye (*ojo*) of a supposéd universality
hovering on the horizon,   a hot air balloon,
    leisure (*ocio*)

        of the landscape's gradual transformation
between so many once opposed   forms of night and day,
        never landing,
but always watching, wistful. On your flight back
you find a book on Lee Lozano   stuffed into the
    seat pocket
        along with a copy of Skymall and
        a pamphlet illustrating emergency
    escape procedures.

        Through the oval window
you watch the sunset and know it was
        the quattrocento
and the troubadours of Provence
had long been dead, never to sing again.

No more
golden *vers, sirventes* and *amour courtois.*
Guillem IX, a sleeping cat; Arnaut Daniel, an ox unyoked.
    Jaufré Rudel

who fell in love with a countess from rumors
       of her beauty, he left on a ship
    for Tripoli
to meet her. He became ill having nearly reached
the city. It was clear he would die, so
    his men
thought it best to grant him a vision
of what he sought. To his room
    the barmaid

       they brought, bedecked in craftily
improvised adornments, said she was the countess come
    to see
him, whereupon he sighed and claimed it was all
as he imagined, then breathed his last in
    her arms.
This barmaid, terrified conscript in this
pathetic deception, after a moment of silence,
    she swore

and cursed them all. When finally free
       from this madman's delusion, from
    the room's
miasma of decadent Romance, death,
      she left the inn and became
    a nun,
averse to all men, ensconced in a convent
      like a lightbulb   beneath a cone
    of lampshade:

"Yo deseo estar solo. Non curo de compaña.
[…] Quiero catar silencio, mi sóla golosina.
     […] dejádme solo."
It was the end of the quattrocento and all that
was left of the troubadours and their influence
     in Spain
were the *Cancioneros*—they did not believe
in St. Francis ("God's troubadour"), no
     divine gifts,

aspired to be understood, their only capacity
for understanding held the court—the forms,
     the gestures
of a foreign love, old allusions and metaphors
formulaic as the punchline of a déclassé joke,
     cheap target
in a dim bar after a day of work, you
asked about his day who says, *Oh, you know,*
     fine.

NOTES

pg. 3 & 25: The Verrazzano-Narrows Bridge, completed in 1964, connects Brooklyn and Staten Island over the tidal straight that is the maritime gateway to New York City. It is named after the Italian explorer Giovanni da Verrazzano. At the time of its inauguration, the name of the bridge was misspelled, with only one 'z,' and it was not officially renamed with the correct double-z spelling until October 2018.

pg. 4: Ian Hamilton Finlay (1925-2006), Scottish poet, artist and gardener. The work referenced here is *Sea Poppy I* (1966).

pg. 7: Joe Brainard (1942-1994), American artist and writer. His most widely read literary work is *I Remember* (Angel Hair, 1970).

pg. 11: Alejandro Otero (1921-1990), Venezuelan painter and sculptor. Well known for his contributions to Op Art and Kinetic Art, the work referenced here is his series of *Coloritmo* paintings (1955-1960).

pg. 12: Leandro Katz (b. 1938), Argentinian writer, artist and filmmaker. *The Lunar Alphabet II* (1980) is a work that substitutes letters of the alphabet with photographs of the phases of the moon. Katz put his lunar alphabet to use in coding *Lunar Sentence II*:

> WHEN WE PULVERIZE WORDS, WHAT IS LEFT IS NEITHER MERE NOISE NOR ARBITRARY, PURE ELEMENTS, BUT STILL OTHER WORDS, REFLECTION OF AN INVISIBLE AND YET INDELIBLE REPRESENTATION: THIS IS THE MYTH IN WHICH WE NOW TRANSCRIBE THE MOST OBSCURE AND REAL POWERS OF LANGUAGE.

pg. 12: *Nadaísta*: of or related to *Nadaísmo*, a Colombian counter-cultural and literary movement active in the 1960s.

Nadaísmo is characterized by existentialist philosophical themes, an irreverent relationship to earlier Colombian poetry, and an anticlerical politics. It has been described by Armando Romero and other scholars of Colombian literature as a (culturally) violent response to the political violence of the 1950s.

pg. 13: Coyolxauhqui is an Aztec goddess often thought to be associated with the moon. The Coyolxauhqui Disk depicts the dismembered body of the goddess after her defeat by Huitzilopochtli and may have served as a warning to the enemies of Tenochtitlan.

pg. 13: Giacomo Leopardi (1798-1837), Italian poet associated with Romanticism: "What are you doing, moon, up in the sky; / what are you doing, tell me, silent moon?" (trans. Jonathan Galassi)

pg. 14: Leopoldo Lugones (1874-1938), Argentinian poet associated with Latin American *Modernismo*. His book, *Lunario Sentimental* (1909), was used as an intermittent source for some of the language and imagery of this poem.

pg. 16: Barbara Guest (1920-2006), American poet associated with the New York School. *The Poetess* (*The Collected Poems*, p.121) refers to a painting of the same title by Spanish painter Juan Miró (1893-1983).

pg. 17: Bob Kaufman (1925-1986), American poet associated with the Beat movement. He was often credited with coining the term "Beatnik," founded the magazine *Beatitude* with Allen Ginsberg, and famously took an oath of silence after the assassination of John F. Kennedy until the end of the Vietnam War.

pg. 20: Amílcar Osorio (1940-1985), Colombian poet associated with *Nadaísmo*. His only book of poems, *Vana Stanza*, languishes like the unseen statue of a handsome god in a storage room beneath a museum.

pg. 21: Nobuyuki Yuasa (b.1932), Japanese translator and scholar. His translation of Matsuo Bashō's *Narrow Road to the Deep North*, published by Penguin Classics, is perhaps the most widely read English translation of this work.

pg. 21: Kobayashi Issa (1763-1828), Japanese poet and lay Buddhist priest from the Edo period. His most famous collection of haibun, *Oraga Haru*, was translated by Yuasa as *The Year of My Life*.

pg. 23: Octavio Paz (1914-1998), Mexican poet and diplomat. His book-length essay on Mexican identity, *The Labyrinth of Solitude*, begins with a chapter titled, "The Pachuco and Other Extremes."

pg. 28: "La Torre," *The Tower*, is the sixteenth card in the Major Arcana of most Tarot decks.

pg. 44-51: Many of the Spanish phrases in this section of "La Torre" are taken from the poem by canonized saint and mystic poet San Juan de la Cruz (1542-1591), *Vivo sin Vivir en Mi*:

> I live without living in myself, and in this way I hope to die because I am not dying.
> I no longer live in myself, and without God I cannot live, for without Him, and left without myself, what would this life be? It would cause me a thousand deaths because I am waiting for my life, dying because I do not die.
> This life I live is privation from living and thus is constant death until I live with you, my God. Hear what I say: I do not want this life, I die because I do not die.
> In your absence, what life can I have, suffering without death, without the beyond I never saw? I pity myself this strength to persevere, because I die of not dying.
> The fish who leaves the water does not need any help

besides the death he lacks, and in the end, gets the death he deserves. What death could equal my pitiful life? The longer I live the more I die.

When my grief begins to dissipate upon seeing you in the Sacrament, I feel my loss ever more. Unable to cherish you, it's all for further penance, and my malady is so all-consuming, I die because I am not dying.

And if I console myself, Lord, with the hope of seeing you, that I might lose you doubles my pain. Living in such terror, and hoping the way I hope, I die because I do not die.

Remove me from this death, my Lord, and give me life. Do not leave me caught in this narrowing noose. See that I am dying to see you and I hope this way to die, because I am not dying.

(trans. Camilo Roldán)

pg. 53: Lee Lozano (1930-1999), American artist. As part of her project pieces—conceptual works that exist as brief written records in her notebooks—Lozano once took LSD every day for a month, 30 tabs in 30 days, an experiment from which some of her friends claim she never recovered.

pg. 66-67:   Works Cited

Donegan, Cheryl. "All Weapons are Boomerangs." *Modern Painters*, Oct. 2006, p. 76.

Lehrer-Graiwer, Sarah. *Lee Lozano: Dropout Piece.* Afterall Books, 2014.

Lippard, Lucy, editor. *Six Years: The Dematerialization of the Art Object from 1966 to 1972.* University of California, 1997.

Molesworth, Helen. "Tune in, Turn on, Drop out: The Rejection of Lee Lozano." *Art Journal*, Vol., 61, No. 4, 2002, pp. 64-71.

O'Neill-Butler, Lauren. "Public Offering," *Art Journal*, Vol. 69, No. 4, 2010, pp. 129-131.

ACKNOWLEDGMENTS

Thanks to all of the people and institutions who have supported me and made this book possible, including but not limited to the following:

Julie Agoos, Thomas Bane, Andrew Bartels, Alex Batkin, Jess Beck, Anselm Berrigan, Eddie Berrigan, Carlos Camacho, Macgregor Card, Eric Conroe, Corina Copp, Diana Cuartas, Alex Cuff, Ryan Cull, Keturah Cummings, Maria Clara Delgado, Ted Dodson, Rachel Downs, Ian Dreiblatt, Georgia Faust, Daniel B. Friedman, Carmen Giménez Smith, Adjua Gargi Nzinga Greaves, Alina Gregorian, Yasmin Gruss, Anna Gurton-Wachter, Shane Hamby, Mark Harris, MC Hyland, Lisa Jarnot, Mike Lala, Krystal Languell, Lisa Latiano, Ben Lerner, Matt Longabucco, Brendan Lorber, Francisco Lozada, David James Miller, Erin Morrill, Nicholas Naughton, Jennifer Nelson, Daniel Owen, Allyson Paty, Judah Rubin, Kit Schluter, Sara Jane Stoner, Sho Sugita, María Jimena Tafur, Andi Talarico, Roberto Tejada, Luisa Ungar, Connie Voisine, Cathy Wagner, Ken Walker, Sarah Wallen, Stu Watson, Marjorie Welish, Natalie Wetzel, and Wendy Xu.

Special thanks to my parents and my brother for their love and support: Janet Millard, Luis Roldán, and Jerónimo Roldán.

Some of the poems in this book previously appeared in the following publications:

Aufgabe, Black Sun Lit, Brooklyn Poets, The Brooklyn Rail, Dreginald, Easy Paradise, Love within Love, The Poetry Project Newsletter, Prelude Magazine, Quaderna, Set, Tammy, and *West Wind Review.*

Well Greased Press published "La Torre" as a chapbook in 2015.